Rocks and Minerals Activity Book

Author	Ellen Sussman
Editor	Kathy Rogers
Illustrator	Barb Lorseyedi
Page Design	Linda Milliken
Cover Design	Imaginings

METRIC CONVERSION CHART

Refer to this chart when metric conversions are not found within the activity.

¼ tsp	=	1 ml	350° F	=	180° C
½ tsp	=	2 ml	375° F	=	190° C
1 tsp	=	5 ml	400° F	=	200° C
1 Tbsp	=	15 ml	425° F	=	216° C
¼ cup	=	60 ml	1 inch	=	2.54 cm
⅓ cup	=	80 ml	1 foot	=	30 cm
½ cup	=	125 ml	1 yard	=	91 cm
1 cup	=	250 ml	1 mile	=	1.6 km
1 oz.	=	28 g			
1 lb.	=	.45 kg			

EP121 • ©1998, 2002 Edupress, Inc.™ • P.O. Box 883 • Dana Point, CA 92629
www.edupressinc.com
ISBN 1-56472-121-3
Printed in USA

Table of Contents

Glossary

boulder—a large stone moved by nature from its original bed.

calcite—a mineral which is in limestone, marble, and chalk.

crust—the rocky, uppermost layer of the Earth.

eruption—the bursting forth of lava from a volcano.

extrusive rock—rock formed from lava after it has reached the surface of the Earth.

facet—any of the many polished sides of a cut gemstone.

feldspar—a mineral found in igneous rocks.

gem—a precious, rare, and perfect stone, especially when set as an ornament.

granite—an abundant, strong, durable igneous rock useful in the construction of buildings and monuments.

hardness—the measurement of how easily a mineral is scratched.

igneous rock—rock formed from magma as it cools and hardens.

intrusive rock—rock formed when magma works its way between rocks and hardens beneath the surface of the Earth.

jewel—a precious stone or gem, especially one set in precious metal.

lava—melted rock that pours out onto the surface of the Earth from a volcano.

limestone—a type of sedimentary rock made from seashells and tiny sea animals which makes an excellent building material because it can be carved easily.

magma—melted rock beneath the Earth's surface.

metamorphic rock—rock created when igneous or sedimentary rock is changed by heat and pressure.

minerals—natural substances that make up rocks and have a chemical composition and a crystalline structure.

pebble—a small, rounded fragment of rock.

pumice—an igneous rock formed from cooled lava that is light and contains air bubbles.

quartz—a common, very hard mineral found in all three major types of rocks.

rock—a natural solid material that makes up the Earth's crust, usually consisting of a mixture of minerals.

sand—a hard, granular rock material that is smaller than gravel and larger than silt.

sedimentary rock—rock formed from many layers of sand, mud, rock fragments and plant and animal remains that have undergone pressure from above.

stalactite—a limestone formation found in some caves that hangs down from the ceiling and is formed when ground water, rich in carbon dioxide, dissolves the mineral calcite from limestone directly above.

stalagmite—a limestone formation found in some caves that rises up from the floor and is formed when water, dripping on the floor, carries with it deposits of calcite.

stone—a small piece of rock.

strata—layers of rock.

volcano—an opening in the Earth's crust through which lava, dust, and hot gases are spewed out.

3

© Edupress EP121

Glossary Game

You have learned a lot about rocks and minerals. See if you know what these words mean. Draw a line to connect each word to its definition.

igneous rock	an opening in the Earth's crust through which lava, dust, and hot gases are spewed out
metamorphic rock	melted rock that pours out onto the surface of the Earth from a volcano
sedimentary rock	layers of rock
intrusive rock	natural substances that make up rocks and have a chemical composition and a crystalline structure
extrusive rock	an igneous rock formed from cooled lava that is light and contains air bubbles
volcano	rock formed from many layers of sand, mud, rock fragments and plant and animal remains that have undergone pressure from above
magma	a natural solid material that makes up the Earth's crust
lava	melted rock beneath the Earth's surface
pumice	rock created when igneous or sedimentary rock is changed by heat and pressure
strata	rock formed from magma as it cools and hardens
rock	rock formed when magma works its way between rocks and hardens beneath the surface of the Earth
minerals	rock formed from lava after it has reached the surface of the Earth

Score: If you got all 12 correct, you are a rock hound!
If you got 10-11 correct, you're a hot rocker!
If you got 9 or fewer correct, you're not rock bottom yet!

4

© Edupress EP121

Introduction

The Earth's crust is made up of several kinds of rocks—each formed in a different way. Some rocks form from red-hot lava that spews from an erupting volcano; others form from rock debris as it is swept down from mountains by rushing waters; and still other rock is formed from the fossils of ancient sea creatures. No matter how the rocks are formed, they are all made up of collections of minerals usually packed haphazardly together and appearing as glassy crystals.

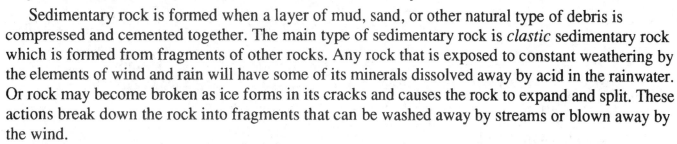

Igneous rock may be the most easily understood type of rock. Molten material from inside the Earth becomes lava once it comes out of a volcano. Once it cools and becomes a solid mass, it is extrusive igneous rock, meaning it cools on the surface of a lava flow. Intrusive igneous rock is formed when molten material becomes imbedded into the rocks of the crust and solidifies there before reaching the surface. This type of intrusive igneous rock can only be seen when the rocks above it have been eroded away.

Sedimentary rock is formed when a layer of mud, sand, or other natural type of debris is compressed and cemented together. The main type of sedimentary rock is *clastic* sedimentary rock which is formed from fragments of other rocks. Any rock that is exposed to constant weathering by the elements of wind and rain will have some of its minerals dissolved away by acid in the rainwater. Or rock may become broken as ice forms in its cracks and causes the rock to expand and split. These actions break down the rock into fragments that can be washed away by streams or blown away by the wind.

Large fragments settle as boulders at the foot of a cliff or shoreline; smaller pieces like silt and sand can travel farther and end up on beaches; and the finest fragments of rock may be washed out to sea and settle as mud. All of these sediments eventually become sedimentary rock such as shale, sandstone, and conglomerate.

Another group of sedimentary rock is *biogenic* sedimentary rock. It is formed from fragments of matter that was once alive, such as corals or seashells. These form limestones and the fossils that originally formed them can frequently be seen in them.

Metamorphic rock is formed when rock is subjected to enormous heat and pressure inside the Earth's crust causing its minerals to change. There are two main types of metamorphic rock—*thermal* metamorphic rock which is formed principally by heat and *regional* metamorphic rock formed mainly by pressure. New minerals may form in contorted layers and bands that correspond to the direction of the pressure. Slate is an example of metamorphic rock and one of the few that is economically valuable.

Individual minerals within a rock are often hard to identify by looking at them with the naked eye. Color is not a valid guide as impurities can change the color of a mineral. A valid method of identifying minerals is the "hardness" test. Since some minerals are harder than others, they can be tested by scratching a sample against others of known hardness. A mineral can only scratch another mineral that is softer than it is.

The streak of a mineral is very distinctive. If a sample of mineral is scraped over a hard surface, it will leave a streak of fine powder containing a color that is constant for a particular mineral even though it may contain impurities.

Minerals are identified by geologists according to their luster, the way they fracture, the shapes of their crystals, as well as their hardness. When light shines on a mineral, it may have a metallic, glassy, or dull luster. When a mineral fractures or breaks, the face may be straight, ragged, or shell-like. Identifying minerals within a rock is a complex task. Geologists use special microscopes to examine a paper-thin, transparent slice of rock to identify the mineral makeup.

Rock Samples

Many of the activities in this book require rock samples. Some items, like sand and marble tiles, can be found at building centers. Other samples can be purchased at hobby or lapidary stores. Natural history museums often have rock and mineral samples for sale at reasonable prices.

Project

Begin your study of Rocks and Minerals by making a list of how rocks and minerals are used.

Materials

- Butcher paper
- Marker

Directions

1. As a class, brainstorm a list of things that people use rocks for, or ways that rocks are part of our lives (i.e., made into concrete, to climb).

2. Once the list has been compiled, make one copy on butcher paper to be posted on the bulletin board for reference during the Rocks and Minerals study.

Our Rocky World

Information

No matter where on Earth you live, you live on rock. Rock is under our city streets and under our country roads. Rock is under every river, lake, stream, and ocean.

The rocks that make up the surface of the Earth are called the Earth's crust. Most of the crust is made of igneous rock. If the Earth could be sliced open, you would see many different layers of rock all packed together.

At one time people thought the Earth was a solid ball. Now we know there are many layers under the crust, and not all of these layers are solid ones. The mantle that lies directly below the crust is a thick layer of solid rock. Below that is the outer core which is a layer of molten rock called magma. The inner core, at the Earth's center, is solid rock.

Project

- Examine an onion and an apple to understand the Earth's layers.
- Draw and label a diagram of the Earth's layers.

Directions

1. Examine the whole onion and imagine it as a model for the Earth.
2. Compare the center of the onion to the Earth's inner core which is made up of solid rocks. Examine the layers of the onion slices. Note the varying thicknesses. Compare this to a three-dimensional model of the Earth.
3. Have an adult cut the apple in half. Observe its center, or core, which is its innermost part. Compare the core to the Earth's inner core.
4. Examine the layer of skin on the apple. The skin is only a very, very thin part of the apple. Compare the skin to the Earth's crust.
5. Complete a diagram of the Earth's layers, labeling each layer and coloring it with the appropriate colors.

Materials

- Whole onion
- Onion slices
- Large apple
- Knife for slicing
- Pencil and paper
- Colored pencils or crayons
- Diagram of Earth's layers, below

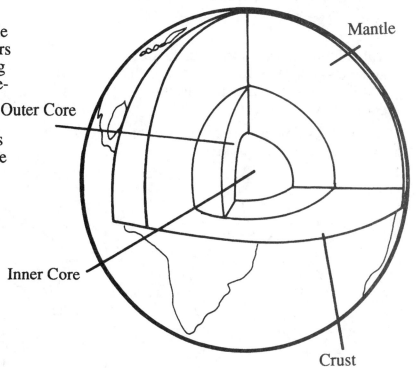

Rocks All Around

Get excited about rocks and minerals by going out and pretending to be amateur geologists! Check out some local sites near the school where you are welcome to search for and collect some specimen rocks. Look around the classroom, the school building, the playground. What is made from rocks or minerals? Discuss chalkboards that used to be made of slate. Does anyone have an old-fashioned slate blackboard at home?

Project

- Participate in a class rock-hunting expedition.
- Create a classroom rock collection with the collected specimens.

Directions

1. Look for and collect unusual rocks in varying sizes.

2. Upon returning to class, clean rocks with an old toothbrush.

3. Compare the samples brought back with photographs of rocks in resource books. Label those which can easily be identified.

4. Talk about shape, color, texture, size, and weight of the samples. Brainstorm a list of ways to organize the display, perhaps by size or color.

5. Set up a display of the class collection.

Materials

- One or more magnifying glasses
- Newspaper or newsprint for wrapping rock specimens
- Goggles (to wear when chipping at rocks)
- A sturdy carton for carrying samples back to school
- Resource books on rock identification
- Labels or index cards
- Marking pens
- Hammers
- Toothbrush

Igneous Rocks

Information

Deep inside the crust of the Earth rocks get so hot they melt. The melted rock is called magma. Sometimes the magma pushes through cracks in the Earth's crust and comes to the surface. Then it is known as *lava*.

Heat, steam, and pressure may build up inside the Earth and cause a volcano to erupt. The melted rock will be forced out of a volcano through a hole called a vent. The melted rock, or lava, cools quickly and becomes very hard volcanic rock known as igneous. The word igneous means "full of fire."

Most of the Earth's igneous rock comes from volcanoes. Granite, basalt, obsidian, and pumice are types of igneous rocks.

Project

Make a model of an erupting volcano.

Materials

- Red food coloring
- A small bottle with a narrow neck
- Modeling clay
- Funnel
- Measuring cup
- Spoon
- One-pound (454 g) box of baking soda
- One-quart (946 ml) bottle of white vinegar
- Plastic or cardboard piece to work on
- Plastic protective apron

Directions

1. Place the bottle in the center of a protected work surface. Remove the cap from the bottle.

2. Place flat pieces of modeling clay around the bottle to create the shape of a volcano. DO NOT cover the opening of the bottle.

3. Pour about ½ cup (50 g) of baking soda into the bottle using the funnel. Fill the bottle halfway; add more baking soda if needed.

4. Add a few drops of red food coloring into ½ cup (118 ml) of vinegar. Stir well.

5. Carefully pour some of the colored vinegar solution into the opening of the volcano— and stand back!

6. Without adding any more baking soda, make the volcano erupt again by pouring more vinegar into the opening when the "lava" stops flowing. Observe where the lava flows. Does it flow in the same direction each time you make the volcano erupt? What effect would a volcano like this have on the land, homes, and people nearby.

7. How is this volcano similar to a real one? How is it different?

8. Clean up your project area using Lava® soap!

Obsidian and Granite

Information

Obsidian is smooth, glossy, and sharp, and looks very much like black glass. It was made by lava that was thrown into the air as a volcano erupted. It cooled very quickly and crystals did not have time to grow. Primitive people used obsidian to make arrowheads and tools. When obsidian is chipped, it can be formed into points with sharp edges. Archeologists can figure out how long ago people lived in certain places by examining objects made of obsidian found at ancient native American sites.

Granite is a volcanic igneous rock that cooled very slowly—perhaps over thousands of years—allowing larger crystals to grow. It is a very abundant igneous rock. As it cools, mineral crystals of feldspar, quartz, and mica have time to grow.

Project

Compare the texture and appearance of obsidian and granite.

Materials

- Samples of obsidian and granite (if unavailable, photographs can be used)
- Magnifying glass
- Paper
- Pencils

Directions

1. Examine the obsidian sample with and without the magnifying glass. Touch and feel the smooth surface. Can you see individual crystals or other formations in the obsidian?

2. Examine the large crystals in a sample of coarse-grained granite with the naked eye and using a magnifying glass. Can you see the speckles and sparkles of various minerals in the rock?

3. In small groups, make a chart comparing the properties of the two types of rock. Include comments on color, texture, and hardness. Brainstorm a list of possible uses for both types of rock.

Obsidian and Granite

Granite comes in many colors, shapes, and textures. People have found it useful for a lot of things. In South Dakota, a sculpture of four United States presidents—George Washington, Thomas Jefferson, Theodore Roosevelt, and Abraham Lincoln—has been carved in the granite cliffs of Mount Rushmore. The sculpture was designed by Gutzon Borglum and is 60 feet (18 m) high. The monument was shaped by blasting away more than 450,000 tons (457,000 metric tons) of granite, one section at a time, with dynamite.

Project

Duplicate the texture and color of granite using crayons or colored pencils and paper.

Materials

- One or more samples or photographs of granite
- White paper
- Crayons or colored pencils

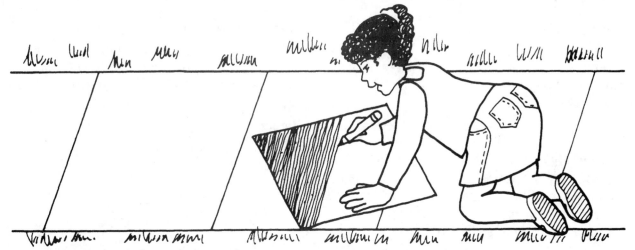

Directions

1. Find a flat but rough cement sidewalk or any flat concrete surface. Clean off any loose pieces of dirt and debris.

2. Examine the rock samples or photographs to determine what colors can be found in the granite. Select crayons or colored pencils to duplicate the colors found.

3. Place a sheet of white paper on the cement. Use one hand to hold the paper firmly in place as you gently and evenly color over most of the paper. Use a light or medium color for the first layer.

4. Move the paper to a slightly different position so the bumps are not in the same places. Repeat and color again using a different color. Remember to color evenly and to hold the paper firmly with one hand.

5. Continue this process, moving the paper three or four times, using a different color crayon or colored pencil each time. Stop when the paper resembles the granite sample or photograph.

11

Pumice and Basalt

Information

Pumice is an igneous rock formed primarily from explosive volcanic eruptions. When gas-filled lava spews into the air, the gas bubbles expand and the frothy lava cools and hardens into pumice. The rock is usually a light gray color and looks like frozen foam. The name pumice comes from a Latin word meaning foam. Since pumice has many air spaces in it, it is very light in weight and can float on water.

Basalt is the most common rock that comes from volcanoes. It forms the cone of the volcano and covers the surrounding land. After many eruptions and lava flows, basalt can accumulate to thousands of feet in thickness. A layer of basalt lies beneath all the ocean floors which make up two-thirds of the Earth's surface. The buildup of basalt from underwater volcanoes can create chains of islands such as the Hawaiian islands.

Project

- Perform an experiment to see which igneous rocks can float.
- Complete a scientific comparison to identify the qualities of different igneous rocks.

Materials

- Large plastic tub or basin of water
- Samples of obsidian, granite, pumice, and basalt, each approximately the same size
- Several samples of pumice in different sizes
- Resource books
- Pencil
- Rock description sheet, following

Directions

1. Pick up the four samples of igneous rocks and arrange them in order of their weight. Which sample feels heaviest? Which sample feels lightest? Which samples do you think may be able to float on water?

2. In groups of four or five, work together to see which of the four types of rocks will float. What conclusions can you reach? What is special about pumice that makes it float?

3. Using the different-sized samples of pumice, experiment to see if all the samples will float or just the smaller ones. Are the larger pumice samples notably heavier than the smaller samples?

4. Based on your observations and information from resource books, complete the rock description sheet to identify the differing qualities of igneous rocks.

Igneous Rock Comparisons

Obsidian

What is its color? _____

_____

Describe its texture. _____

_____

What minerals might it contain? _____

_____

Describe its qualities and appearance. _____

_____

_____

_____

Granite

What is its color? _____

_____

Describe its texture. _____

_____

What minerals might it contain? _____

_____

Describe its qualities and appearance. _____

_____

_____

_____

Pumice

What is its color? _____

_____

Describe its texture. _____

_____

What minerals might it contain? _____

_____

Describe its qualities and appearance. _____

_____

_____

_____

Basalt

What is its color? _____

_____

Describe its texture. _____

_____

What minerals might it contain? _____

_____

Describe its qualities and appearance. _____

_____

_____

_____

Rocks & Minerals Activity Book

Sedimentary Rocks

Information

Sedimentary rock forms as nature carries loose bits of soil, pebbles, sand, and clay, along with animal and plant material, and deposits them in lakes and oceans.

Most sedimentary rock forms under water. Rivers carry sand and mud which can travel all the way to the ocean before it gradually settles to the bottom. The process takes millions of years as sediment is slowly buried by more layers of sediment piling on top. As the pile gets heavier, the particles near the bottom are squeezed closer together. As this is happening, it is warmed by the heat of the Earth. Ground water brings minerals which act as a cement to bond all the particles together and sedimentary rock is formed.

Sandstone, limestone, and shale are types of sedimentary rocks.

Project

Demonstrate how layers of sedimentary rock are formed.

Materials

- Sand
- Plaster of Paris
- Three different colors of food coloring
- Plastic bottle with the top cut off
- Small seashells for fossils
- Bowl
- Spoon
- Water
- Petroleum jelly

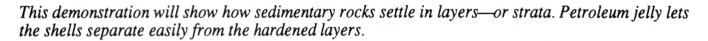

Directions

This demonstration will show how sedimentary rocks settle in layers—or strata. Petroleum jelly lets the shells separate easily from the hardened layers.

1. Put equal amounts of plaster of Paris and sand into a bowl. Use at least ½ cup (118 ml) of each. Add a few drops of food coloring and just enough water to make a smooth paste.

2. Pour or spoon this mixture into the plastic bottle.

3. Rub some petroleum jelly onto a seashell and drop it in the bottle. This will act as a "fossil."

4. Repeat this process using a different food coloring and adding more seashells. Rub petroleum jelly onto each seashell before placing it on the next layer.

5. Build up three or more layers in the bottle. Let the layers harden for several days.

6. When the mixture appears dry, gently cut away the plastic bottle from the hardened layers.

7. Break open the layers and observe the "fossils" and their imprints in the "sedimentary rock."

Rocks Under Pressure

Information

The mystery of how solid rocks are reheated and metamorphosed was solved only a few decades ago. Geologists found that the Earth's plates slide and crunch into one another regularly. This happens in different ways.

When two plates collide, the rocks at the edges of the plates are squeezed. This causes *metamorphosis*. When one plate is forced under another one, it may be plunged into the hot mantle in the Earth. When magma rises, it heats and causes changes in the older rock around it. Earth movements can twist and fold layers into new shapes.

You might think of metamorphic rock as being "baked" under heat and high pressure. Rocks ten miles (16 km) below the surface at temperatures of 700°F (370°C) are subjected to enormous pressure. Not surprisingly, the minerals change, and the squeezing caused by pressure forms new layers and wavy shapes in some rocks.

Project

Conduct two experiments to explore how heat and pressure change the way things look and feel.

Directions

If your area gets snow, try this experiment on the next snowy day! If your area doesn't get snow, try using shaved ice.

1. Make snowballs from light, fluffy snow.

2. Apply pressure by squeezing snowballs as hard as possible. Observe as the compressed snow crystals melt and come together to form a hard and heavy snowball.

3. What conclusions can you draw about how this happens? What causes the snowball to become harder and denser than the fluffy snow?

Materials

- Snow or shaved ice
- Gloves
- Three or four colors of modeling clay
- Rolling pin
- Knife

Rocks Under Pressure

As sedimentary rock layers form one on top of another, the oldest layer is at the bottom. But movements in the Earth can twist and fold layers into new shapes.

Try this experiment to explore how the process works. What conclusions can you draw about the effects of movement upon the Earth's layers.

Roll a piece of modeling clay into a flat sheet. This bottom sheet will be the oldest layer of rock.

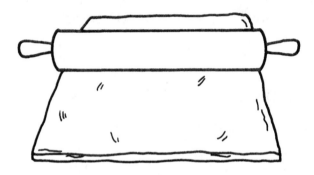

Repeat with the other colors of clay. Press each layer onto the one below it.

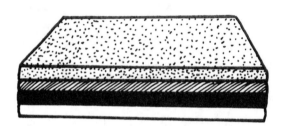

Once you have four different-colored layers, push the two ends toward each other to push up a mountain shape.

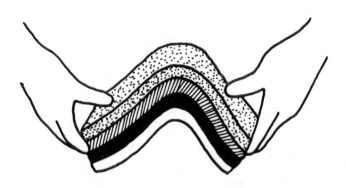

Slice off the top with a knife. The layers that were horizontal can now be seen vertically.

Have you seen mountains like this? What do they look like when the side is exposed to view? Look in resource books for pictures of this type of mountain and make a sketch of your own. Color the different layers. Compare your sketch and the photograph to the clay model. Display your sketch and the model together.

Rocks & Minerals Activity Book

Sandstone

Information

As its name suggests, *sandstone* is made from grains of sand that have been cemented together to form stone. It is often a soft and grainy rock. When you rub sandstone with your fingers, grains of sand may come off. Its color and strength depends on the material that cements it together. Silica provides the strongest cement.

The different minerals in sandstone make it red, yellow, tan, brown, or gray. Sandstone with iron oxide is a reddish-rust color from the iron. You can see different colored layers of sandstone on the cliffs and canyons in Capitol Reef National Park and Monument Valley in Utah. Sandstone is found where ancient seas used to exist.

Project

Conduct a demonstration to show how sandstone is formed.

Materials

- ½ cup (118 ml) water
- ½ cup (118 ml) dry sand, available at a building supply store
- Two paper cups
- 2½ tablespoons (37 ml) Epsom salts
- Spoon

Directions

Start this experiment in the morning as the process in step 4 needs to be repeated several times during the first day.

1. Place about 1½ inches (4 cm) of water in one paper cup.

2. Add the Epsom salts to the water and stir continuously until almost all the salt has been absorbed. (The salts will cement the grains of sand together as minerals cement sand particles together in real sandstone.)

3. Put 1½ inches (4 cm) of dry sand into the second cup. Pour the salt mixture into the sand and stir together until the sand is completely wet.

4. Allow the wet salt/sand mixture to sit for about one hour. Carefully pour off any water that has risen to the top. You will need to do this several times during the first day of this process. Place the paper cup in a dry location where it will not be disturbed for about one week. Leave the paper cup uncovered.

5. When the salt/sand mixture is completely dry, tear the paper cup away from the hardened mixture. If the bottom and sides are still damp, let it sit undisturbed until it is thoroughly dry.

6. When the mixture is completely dry, it should feel like real sandstone. Feel its texture. Compare with a sample of real sandstone.

Limestone

Information

Limestone is a type of sedimentary rock made from seashells and tiny sea animals. You can sometimes see pieces of fossilized shells in shell limestone. Limestone is used to make cement. The limestone is mixed with sand, gravel, and water to make concrete for sidewalks.

Over 5,000 years ago, the pyramids were built in Egypt out of limestone. They are still standing! The chalk you draw with is a kind of limestone. It is the microscopic remains of tiny creatures that lived in the seas during the Cretaceous period of the Earth's history—about 150 million years ago! "Cretaceous" means chalky. Chalk belongs to a group of minerals called carbonates, and all carbonates dissolve in acid.

Project

Conduct an experiment to determine whether or not a rock sample is chalk.

Directions

1. Examine the rock samples carefully. Separate them into two piles—those that you think may be chalk and those that you think are not chalk.

2. Place a piece of rock on a glazed plate.

3. Fill the dropper with vinegar. Drip some onto the rock.

4. Look closely at the rock using the magnifying glass. If it is chalk, it will fizz. This happens when the acid in the vinegar reacts with the chalk. Take careful notes of what you observe.

5. Repeat the steps with all of the rock samples. Were you successful in identifying the chalk samples?

Materials

- Strong vinegar
- Medicine dropper
- Magnifying glass
- Glazed plate
- Rock samples, including some that you think might be chalk

Building with Stone

Information

For thousands of years stone has been a natural choice for building. The great pyramids in Egypt were built mostly of limestone from a quarry near Cairo. Because limestone is in plentiful supply, many famous structures are built with it including the Notre Dame Cathedral in Paris. The Taj Mahal in India is built from pure white marble and is decorated with inlaid gems. It stands on a platform of red sandstone. Granite is harder than limestone, sandstone, or marble, and stands up to weather best. It can be polished like marble and is a favorite for skyscrapers.

Many buildings are now constructed mainly of man-made materials such as brick and concrete. These materials originated from rock; brick is made from soft clay that has a been baked and hardened in a kiln, and concrete is a mixture of sand, gravel, ground limestone, and water.

Project

- Conduct an experiment to determine why stone is a good building material.
- Do research to identify the types of stone used in famous world landmarks.
- Carry out a visual survey to identify stone or stone products used in modern homes and other buildings.

Materials

- Samples of limestone, granite, and sandstone rocks
- Marble floor or counter tile
- Piece of stucco
- Small piece of wood
- Dish pan or bucket
- Water

Directions

1. Examine the different building materials. Form a hypothesis about how each material might respond when exposed to sun, heat, and water.

2. Select a spot outdoors where the materials will be exposed to constant sunlight most of the day. Leave the materials outside for five to ten days.

3. Bring the materials indoors and note any changes you see that have taken place.

4. Submerge the samples in water in the dish pan or bucket. Leave for several days, checking periodically to see if any changes have taken place.

5. At the end of the experiment, compare the samples to one another and reach a conclusion about which materials have withstood weathering with the least damage.

Building With Stone

Brownstone, a reddish-brown type of sandstone, was once widely used in building houses in the eastern United States. In New York City, the use of brownstone was so popular that houses made with this type of sandstone were—and still are—referred to simply as brownstones.

Rocks and stone have been used to construct buildings for thousands of years. Builders used local rocks cut into blocks. Nowadays people build with bricks, tiles, and concrete in place of rocks and stone. These modern building materials are easier to cut and shape and are less expensive than quarrying stone.

Take a survey of your community. Are there any homes, buildings, or statues made from stone? What kind of stone are they made from? Take a notebook for making notes and go for a walk in your community with an adult. Look at the different types of buildings. If you see one built of stone, or if stone was used in part of it, see if you can find out what type of stone it is.

Name of Building or Address	What Type of Stone is Used
_____	_____
_____	_____
_____	_____
_____	_____

What is your house or apartment building made from? List all the materials you can see on the inside and outside. Identify the materials that are rock.

Material	Is it rock?
_____	_____
_____	_____
_____	_____
_____	_____

Rocks & Minerals Activity Book

Name That Stone!

Do some research on each of the following famous buildings. Use encyclopedias, library books, and the Internet. What materials were used to build each one?

The Pyramids were built from

_____

The CN Tower in Ontario is built from

_____

The White House is built from

_____

The Taj Mahal was built from

_____

The Empire State Building was built from

_____

The Sydney Opera House was built from

_____

Answer Key
Pyramids: Limestone
White House: Limestone
Empire State Building: Limestone, granite
Sydney Opera House: Concrete (limestone, gravel)
CN Tower: Concrete (limestone, gravel, clay, sand)
Taj Mahal: Marble, sandstone

Metamorphic Rocks

Information

Just as heat causes dough to change into bread in the oven and just as a caterpillar goes through metamorphosis and changes into a butterfly, rocks can also change in appearance and structure from the rock it once was.

Heat and pressure can cause igneous and sedimentary rock to change into metamorphic rock. Heat may be caused by high temperatures of nearby magma, hot gases, or the intense heat deep within the Earth. Pressure may result from the weight of the Earth above or from movement of plates within the Earth's crust. These changes can cause physical and chemical changes in rocks. The new metamorphic rock can differ in hardness, texture, and color from the original rock. Examples of metamorphic rocks include slate, marble, gneiss, and quartzite.

Project

Create an informational display of metamorphic rocks.

Materials

- Samples of metamorphic rocks (several samples of each one)
- Resource books
- Index card
- Pencils

Directions

1. Divide into small groups and select rock samples.

2. Use resource materials to gather information about your samples of metamorphic rocks. Answer these questions about each:
   - What kind of rock was it before metamorphosis?
   - How did it look before?
   - Describe its appearance and qualities now.

3. Use index cards and write one question or riddle about a rock sample on each card. Write the answer on the reverse side.

4. Arrange your rock samples and index cards in an interesting display.

5. Share your display with the other groups.

Metamorphic Rocks

Many of the qualities of metamorphic rocks make them very useful for building and construction. Sandstone can turn into quartzite. It may still look like sedimentary sandstone, but it is much harder as a metamorphic rock. Quartzite is used for roads. Shale can turn into slate. It becomes much harder as it changes. Slate can be split easily into flat pieces and is an ideal stone for roof, floor, and patio or walkway tiles. School blackboards used to be made from slate.

Limestone can turn into marble. Marble is used to make statues. It is soft enough for a sculptor to carve tiny details, but it is very strong. It can be sculpted easily without splitting, and it can be polished to look smooth and shiny. Pure marble is white, but other colors are common due to impurities of minerals. Statuary marble has a special luster from the rock's translucence. Light is able to penetrate the marble just a bit and reflect off the crystal surfaces inside.

Granite can turn into gneiss. It becomes darker as it changes. Its crystals separate into layers as it becomes metamorphic rock.

Project

- Visit a building supply store to learn about rocks used in building.
- Create a sculpture like those done in marble.

Materials

- Soap
- Plastic knife
- Waxed paper

Directions

1. Take a field trip to a building supply store. Ask questions about how stones are used around homes and other buildings. Ask what makes the different types of stone good building material.

2. Select a bar of soap that you think resembles marble. (You might be able to find soap that has a "marbleized" appearance.)

3. Working with a plastic knife over a sheet of waxed paper, carefully sculpt a three-dimensional object from the soap.

4. When you are finished with the sculpting, carefully rub it with your thumb to soften and smooth the cut lines in your sculpture.

5. Set up a classroom display of your "marble" statuary.

Coal

Information

Just as chalk is called white rock, coal is called black rock. Coal is a black rock that can be ignited and burned. The heat from coal can be used to heat buildings and produce electricity. Coal is also used to make coke, an important raw material used in the manufacture of iron and steel.

Coal is formed in a three-step process that takes millions of years:
- The remains of dead plants and stems fall on the forest floor, rot, and turn into peat.
- The peat becomes buried under new layers of mud and rock.
- The buried peat is subjected to great pressure. After millions of years, the peat turns into coal.

Project

Work in small groups to create a vertical illustrated time-line showing how coal is formed.

Directions

1. Layer the samples of small rocks and pebbles, dead plants, and fresh soil to illustrate the stages in the development of coal. Place rocks and pebbles at the bottom to represent coal, dead plants in the middle to represent peat, and place the fresh soil as the top layer.

2. Use resource books to learn further details about the formation of the layers involved in the coal-making process.

3. Set up a large bulletin board with butcher paper. Divide into small groups to illustrate and label the layers showing the development of coal.

Materials

- Resource books about coal
- Butcher paper for mural
- Paints, crayons, and markers
- Dead plants, small rocks, and pebbles
- Fresh soil
- Coal Quiz, following

Answer Key for Coal Quiz
1. Anthracite
2. Coke
3. Pennsylvania, Ohio, West Virginia, Kentucky, Tennessee, Alabama, Michigan, Illinois, Indiana, Iowa, Kansas, Missouri, Oklahoma, Texas, Utah, Colorado, North Dakota, Montana, Wyoming, New Mexico, Arizona
4. Coal beds
5. Russia, China
6. Because it developed from plants that died one to 440 million years ago
7. It is abundant, it has a high heating value
8. Alberta, Saskatchewan, British Columbia
9. Coal auger
10. They are all carbon

Bonus: Because it begins as one kind of rock and is changed by pressure

---

Coal Quiz

Read about coal in resource books from your classroom and library.
Take this "Coal Quiz" and see how much you have learned about coal.

1. What is the hardest type of coal?

2. What is the name of the raw material obtained from coal that is used in the manufacture of iron and steel?

3. List five U.S. states that have large deposits of coal.

4. What is the name of the underground place that coal is found?

5. Name two other countries that are leading coal-producers?

6. Why is coal called a fossil fuel?

7. Give two reasons to explain why coal is a useful fuel.

8. More than 95% of Canada's coal reserves are located in three provinces. Name these provinces.

9. Name the machine that miners use to dig out coal.

10. What does coal have in common with a diamond and a pencil?

Bonus Question! Why do you think coal is a type of metamorphic rock?

Name _____

Crystals

Information

A *crystal* is a solid that is made up of atoms arranged in an orderly pattern. Most substances that are not living are composed of crystals. Metals, rocks, snowflakes, salt, and sugar consist of crystals.

Crystals may form from vapors, solutions, or from melting caused by molten materials deep within the Earth. The intense heat melts minerals in rocks. In time, the minerals cool and harden into new structures called crystals.

Crystals are evenly shaped because they are made up of tiny atoms that arrange themselves in the same regular pattern as the crystal grows.

Project

- Grow salt crystals to observe their characteristics.
- Make rock candy.

Materials

- Salt
- Glass jar
- Pencil
- Strand of yarn
- Warm water

Directions

A crystal grows as layers of its mineral are added to its surface.

1. Fill a jar about two-thirds full of warm water. Add salt and stir. Continue adding more salt and stirring until no more salt will dissolve in the water.

2. Tie a piece of yarn around the middle of the pencil so that the yarn dangles in the water. Set the jar in a cool place.

3. Observe that as the water cools, salt crystals grow on the yarn.

4. Pour off the water each day. Add a fresh amount of dissolved salt to the jar.

5. Observe daily and see the crystals on the yarn get larger. Measure and record the size of the crystal each day.

6. Try doing this experiment by putting a second sample as a control in a warm location. Crystals grow differently in a hot or warm location than they do in a cool location. What difference does the temperature of the location have on the way crystals grow?

26

Make Rock Candy

Project

Here's an activity where you can grow crystals that look pretty and taste good!

Materials

- Two Pyrex® or heat-proof glass jars or bowls
- Pot for cooking
- Dull table knife
- 1 cup (236 ml) granulated sugar
- ½ cup (118 ml) water
- Food coloring (optional)

Directions

1. Pour the sugar into the cooking pot. Add the water, but do not stir the mixture.

2. Bring the mixture to a boil over medium-high heat. Let it boil for one minute without stirring.

3. If you would like to add color to the rock candy, add a few drops of food coloring as the mixture boils.

4. Pour the mixture into one or two glass jars or bowls. (This should be done by an adult!)

5. Let the jars or bowls sit undisturbed for two weeks. Check daily and watch as crystals begin to form.

6. When a crust forms on top, tap it gently with a table knife to break the crust. This will allow the water to continue to evaporate. Otherwise, do not move or disturb the jars in any way.

7. When the crystals have grown to the size you like, break the rock candy from the jar or bowl with a table knife.

8. Enjoy this sweet and tasty crystal treat!

Gems

Information

For a mineral to be considered a gemstone, it must possess certain criteria. It must have perfect crystals, beautiful colors, sparkling lights, and it must be rare. Additionally, it must be very hard.

Gemstones look very different when you see them in a jewelry store than when they were first mined or found by a riverbed. This is because over 400 years ago people found that a gemstone could be made to look more colorful and brilliant by making small, flat cuts called *facets* on the surface of the stone.

By cutting the facets at exact angles, the light that enters a gem is trapped for a short time. The light bounces back and forth inside the gemstone and makes it more brilliant.

Project

Visit a jewelry store to see and learn about precious gems.

Materials

• What A Gem! page, following

Directions

For this activity it is suggested that you plan ahead for a scheduled time when the class may visit a jeweler who can have a representative display and discuss precious gems with the class. If this is not possible, an exhibit at a local natural history museum can be arranged.

1. Prior to visiting the jewelry store, duplicate the following page to gain more information about gemstones.

2. Take a trip to a jeweler. Remember, there is a "hands-off" rule for this field trip!

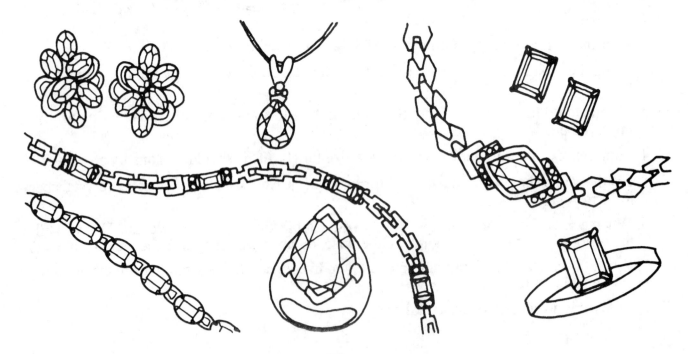

What A Gem!

A diamond is one of the rarest and most valuable gemstones. A diamond is formed from pure carbon which has been subjected to enormous pressure over a long period of time deep down in the Earth's crust. The pressure must be extremely high so that the atoms of carbon are packed just right to form the hard mold of diamond.

An emerald is another very precious gemstone. It is formed from the mineral beryl which is usually a grayish or greenish color. Sometimes beryl has just the right mix of atoms to make the color a brilliant green.

Sapphires and rubies both come from the mineral corundum which contains aluminum and oxygen. With a bit of metal chromium added, corundum becomes a beautiful red ruby. With a bit of iron and titanium added, corundum becomes a brilliant blue sapphire.

Opal is a gem that is like quartz but it doesn't have a crystal structure so it appears more like glass. It may appear in a variety of colors like pearly blue-green, pink, and almost black, but the gem collector's favorite color is milky white.

Project

Create a poster featuring gemstones.

Directions

1. Look through magazines and jewelry advertisements that come in the mail. Cut out photographs of rings, necklaces, and bracelets with gemstones.

2. Glue the pictures to the poster board. Label each gemstone.

Materials

- Magazines, catalogs, advertisements
- Poster board
- Scissors
- Glue

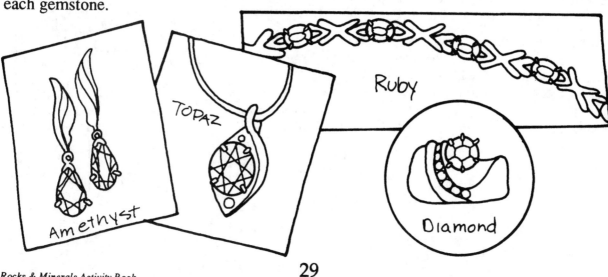

From Gemstones to Jewels

Information

Gemstones are minerals used in jewelry. When a gemstone is first removed from a rock, it usually appears dull.

A gem cutter, or *lapidary*, carefully cuts and polishes the stone to create an object of great value and beauty. Each type of gemstone has a traditional cut shape that shows off its color and sparkle.

Gemstones are valuable because they are rare and are so hard that they almost never scratch. The most valuable gems are diamonds, emeralds, rubies, and sapphires. Although rubies are red and most sapphires are blue, they are both forms of the mineral *corundum*. The red color of the ruby comes from the metal chromium, and the blue color of the sapphire comes from small amounts of titanium and iron.

Project

- Make a graph showing students' birthstones.
- Research to learn about what gemstones are like before they are cut.

Materials

- Resource books
- Full-color chart showing 12 birthstones
- Our Birthstones graph, following
- Crayons, markers, or colored pencils to match birthstone colors

Directions

The tradition of birthstones started over 2,000 years ago! Let each student learn what their birthstone is!

1. Display an illustrated full-color chart showing birthstones. (This may be found in books on rocks and minerals.) Use the graph chart on the following page or make an enlarged version. Color in illustrated birthstones as indicated.

2. Each student uses the chart to find their birthstone, then colors on a square in the chart next to the birthstone name with the appropriate color.

3. Use resource books to find out more about the gemstones represented by the class. Divide into groups, each group selecting a different gemstone. Prepare short reports that include information about where the stones can be found, what kind of rock the stone is usually found in, and what the stone looks like before it is cut.

Rocks & Minerals Activity Book

Our Birthstones

January—Garnet (deep red)
February—Amethyst (medium pink)
March—Aquamarine (light blue)
April—Diamond (clear)
May—Emerald (bright green)
June—Pearl (soft white)
July—Ruby (dark red)
August—Peridot (lime green)
September—Sapphire (deep blue)
October—Opal (blue-green)
November—Topaz (orange-brown)
December—Turquoise (turquoise)

31

Minerals

Information

Rocks contain many different kinds of *minerals*. Some rocks contain only one kind of mineral; others will contain two or more.

Individual minerals can be difficult to identify just by looking at them. Impurities in minerals affect their color; therefore a mineral cannot be positively identified solely by color.

In 1822, a German geologist named Friedrich Mohs invented the *Mohs' Scale of Hardness*. The scale goes from numbers 1 to 10. The softest mineral, talc, is #1. Diamond is the hardest at #10. Any mineral on the scale will scratch any mineral above it. A diamond can scratch all the other minerals because it is the hardest.

Project

Experiment to see which rocks and minerals are harder than others.

Materials

- Mohs' Scale of Hardness, following
- Copper coins or pennies
- Mineral samples

Directions

1. Duplicate the illustrated scale of hardness on the following page. Discuss how any mineral on the scale can scratch the mineral above it. (Remember that the lower the number, the softer the mineral.) Gypsum can scratch talc, topaz can scratch quartz, quartz can scratch feldspar as well as all minerals with a lower number on the scale.

2. If available, obtain a sample piece of talc. See how soft it is by pinching it into powder with your fingers. Test to see how easily it scratches.

3. Set up a table with mineral samples. Experiment to see which samples are harder than others using copper coins and your fingernails. If a rock can be scratched with a fingernail, it has a hardness of less than 2.5. A fingernail can scratch talc and gypsum. If a rock can be scratched with a copper coin, it has a hardness of less than 3.

32

Hard and Soft Minerals

Soft

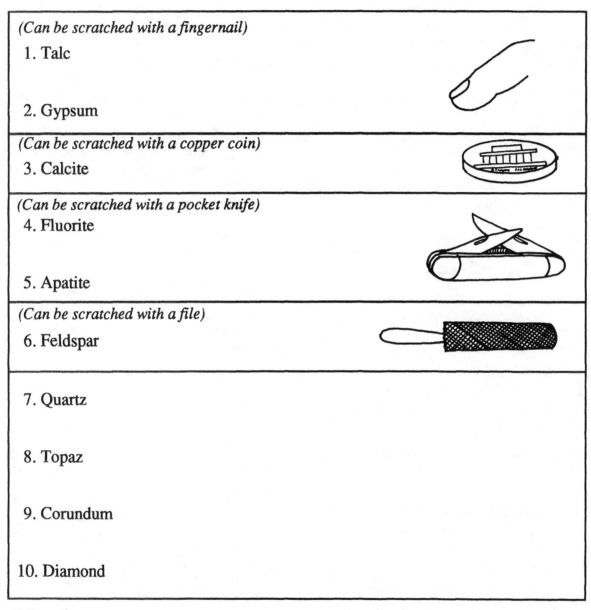

(Can be scratched with a fingernail)

1. Talc

2. Gypsum

(Can be scratched with a copper coin)

3. Calcite

(Can be scratched with a pocket knife)

4. Fluorite

5. Apatite

(Can be scratched with a file)

6. Feldspar

7. Quartz

8. Topaz

9. Corundum

10. Diamond

Hard

Test a number of objects to see where they rate on Mohs' Scale of Hardness. Once you have determined what hardness level an object is, make a note of it in the corresponding box on the chart.

Solve this gem of a question!
If diamond is the hardest mineral, how can you cut a diamond to make diamond jewelry?

Stalactites & Stalagmites

Information

Some sedimentary rocks are formed chemically when minerals dissolved in water are deposited over a long period of time. If water seeps through limestone in the ground, the water will dissolve the mineral calcite from the limestone. As the water evaporates in cracks and caves, the dissolved calcite is left behind.

Stalactites form as water drips *downward* from a ceiling or roof of a cave. As it evaporates it leaves behind minerals—one drop at a time—which gradually form needle-shaped stalactites that hang from the ceiling like icicles.

Stalagmites form when water drops hit the floor of a cave. They build *upward* and form upside-down icicles. Carlsbad Caverns in New Mexico contain some of the most spectacular formations of chemically formed sedimentary rocks of this type in the world.

Project

Create stalactites and stalagmites.

Directions

1. Fill the jars about two-thirds full of warm water. Add some baking soda and stir. Add more baking soda and repeat until no more soda dissolves.

2. Cut an 18-inch (45.7-cm) piece of yarn and weigh down each end by attaching a paper clip.

3. Space the jars about 12 inches (30.5 cm) apart. Place each end of the yarn into one of the jars. Place a dish under the yarn, between the jars.

4. Observe as the baking soda solution seeps along the yarn and drips onto the dish. A stalactite will form on the yarn in a pointed shape that hangs down as the solution drips down. A stalagmite will form on the dish and grow upwards as the drips evaporate and leave deposits.

Materials

- Yarn
- Paper clips
- Spoon
- Two large glass jars
- Baking soda
- Dish

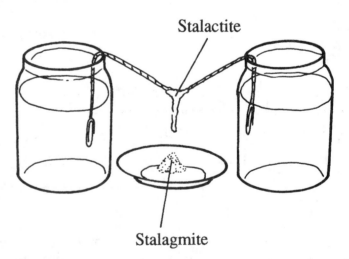

Stalactite

Stalagmite

© Edupress EP121

Famous Formations

Many people find stalactite and stalagmite formations very interesting. The Carlsbad Caverns in southeastern New Mexico became a national park in 1930. These caverns contain stalactites and stalagmite formations that look like Chinese temples, heavy pillars, and lacy icicles. Use resource books to find information and photographs of other famous caves and caverns, challenging yourself to answer the questions below.

One large chamber in Carlsbad Caverns is called the Big Room.

• It is _____ feet (meters) high and _____ feet (meters) wide.

• At one point, the ceiling is _____ feet (meters) high.

Other beautiful examples of stalactites and stalagmites in the United States can be found in:

_____ Caverns in _____

_____ Caverns in _____

_____ Caverns in _____

_____ Caverns in _____

_____ Caverns in _____

Look at this map of the United States. Color in the five states that have famous caverns filled with stalactites and stalagmites.

Source: World Book Encyclopedia

© Edupress EP121

Precious Metals

Information

Some minerals are considered valuable because they are very hard to find and can be used to make many types of very useful products. Some minerals—metals, for example—have hundreds of different uses. Other minerals—such as gemstones—are used mostly in jewelry.

There are some minerals that are dug out of mines, crushed, and melted to remove the useful metal such as iron, copper, and tin. The metals are used to make batteries, pipes, pots and pans, automobiles, trains, airplanes, and many other items.

Platinum, silver, and gold are rare and valuable metals used to make coins and jewelry. These metals glitter and shine; they are soft enough to shape easily; and they don't lose their beauty or rust over the years.

Project

Learn important facts about metals by making a "Precious Metals Primer."

Materials

- Precious Metals Primer pages, following
- Mail-order catalogs, magazines
- Scissors
- Stapler
- Glue

Directions

1. Reproduce the pattern pages and cut them apart. Staple the pages together in book form.

2. Look through catalogs and magazines for pictures of items, as listed in the primer pages, made from precious metals.

3. Cut the pictures out and glue them to the appropriate pages.

4. Use the book as a basis of discussion for the many useful purposes of metals.

Precious Metals Primer

Aluminum is the third most common element in the Earth's crust, and it is the most common metal. Aluminum is most easily removed from rock called *bauxite*. Aluminum from bauxite ore is strong and lightweight. It is used for building, automobiles, airplanes, foil, pots and pans, and has many other uses.

Copper is used mainly for making water pipes and wire. It is also used to make cooking pots because it is a good conductor of heat. Copper, when mixed with zinc, makes an alloy called *brass*. Copper ores are brilliant in color. Azurite is blue, malachite is green, and chalcopyrite is gold.

Iron is a very important precious metal. It is strong and hard but it melts easily so it can be poured into molds and flattened into sheets. When combined with carbon and other elements, iron forms alloys such as wrought iron, cast iron, and steel, which is the most-used metal in the world. The main iron ore is called *hematite*.

Lead is made from a shiny black mineral known as *galena* that is often found in limestone and silver. Lead is used in materials to protect people against x-rays and radioactivity. Lead is also used in making batteries. Lead is a very heavy metal.

Mercury is the only metal that is in a liquid form even when it is not hot. It comes from a red ore called *cinnabar* and is found only in a few places in the world, including Italy, Spain, and the western part of the United States. Mercury is used in thermometers and barometers and as an ingredient in paint and some medicines.

Nickel is a strong metal that can stand up to hard wear and high temperatures. Its main use is to add strength to steel. The main nickel ores are *pyrrhotite* and *pentlandite*. Nickel is also mixed with copper to make coins. The U.S. nickel has three times more copper than nickel!

Tin is used mostly in making products such as tin cans. It comes from a hard and heavy ore called *cassiterite*. Tin is mixed with copper to make bronze and is mixed with lead to make pewter.

Rocks & Minerals Activity Book   © Edupress EP121

Zinc is used to make brass and to give metals a protective coating. It comes from an ore called *sphalerite*. The rock is generally black but can also be green, yellow, or red, which makes it difficult to identify.

Gold is the most workable of all the precious metals. It can be hammered into very thin sheets called *gold leaf*, stretched to make thin wire for chains, and molded into almost any shape. It is used to make coins and jewelry. Gold is usually found in veins (or cracks) of quartz and does not have to be processed as many other metals do.

Platinum doesn't tarnish like silver but it doesn't have the gleam and shine of gold either. It is more valuable than gold in some ways because it is in great demand in the oil refining industry and in making low-pollution car exhaust systems. It is also used for jewelry. In the days of Czar Nicholas I, three-ruble Russian coins were made of platinum.

Silver is a less precious metal than gold because its surface reacts with air and causes the metal to tarnish or darken. It has to be polished occasionally to remove the tarnish and bring back its natural shine. Silver is used for fine tableware, jewelry, and coins. More than one-third of all silver mined in the United States is used for making and developing photographic film. Silver is found as a native metal or in ore known as *argentite*.

© Edupress EP121

Metals and Man

Information

Minerals with large amounts of metals that can be easily separated are called *ore minerals*. These rocks are mined from the Earth's crust or dredged out of lakes and streams. The ore is crushed and the metal is removed from the rock. Then it is heated, or smelted, to make pure metal. About 4,000 years ago, metalworkers learned to mine rock that contained iron—a very strong metal that could be sharpened easily. They heated the ore in a forge until the iron was separated from the rock. Once cooled, the iron could be hammered and shaped into tools and weapons. This was the beginning of The Iron Age.

Project

- Brainstorm a list of tools made in the Iron Age.
- Make replicas of Iron Age tools and set up a display explaining the tools' use.

Materials

- Resource books
- Poster board
- Scissors or Exacto® Knife
- Aluminum foil
- Index cards
- Pencil or pen

Directions

1. During the Iron Age, man learned to make many tools from metal that had been made from softer substances. Use resource books to find out what these tools were and how they were used.

2. Use scissors or Exacto® knife to cut tool shapes from poster board. Cover the shapes with aluminum foil.

3. Write the name of your tool on an index card. Write a paragraph that explains the use of the tool and why it was a better tool because it was made of metal. Was the same tool made of something else prior to the Iron Age?

POINTER   SCRAPER   GRINDER

Rocks & Minerals Activity Book   © Edupress EP121

Sand

Information

Sand is any earth material consisting of loose grains of minerals or rocks larger than silt but smaller than gravel. Geologists measure sand by shaking it through a very fine wire mesh or screen.

Most grains of sand come from solid rocks that have crumbled away as the rock breaks down from forces of air, water, ocean waves, and frost.

Geologists find many types of minerals in sand, but the most common mineral is quartz. Sand found on beaches of many Pacific islands consists of basalt grains from volcanic activity.

Sand is used to make chemicals and glass. It is also used in mortar and concrete.

Project

- Discover what sand is made of.
- Make and explore the properties of sandpaper.

Materials

- Rocks and sand
- Magnifying glass
- Magnet
- Shallow gift or pizza boxes

Directions

1. Fill a large shallow box with sand.

2. Observe, feel, and look at the sand. What differences can you see in the grains of sand?

3. Examine grains of sand by looking through a magnifying glass. Do the grains vary in size, shape, or color?

4. Brainstorm a list of ways that sand might be made.

5. Rub two rocks together, collecting the resulting debris. Examine the debris to see if it resembles sand. Use a magnet to determine whether the hand-made sand contains any iron.

41

Working With Sandpaper

Do you or your parents use sandpaper at home? What do you use it for? How do you think sandpaper is made? Examine pieces of sandpaper and compare them to one another. How are the pieces of sandpaper different from each other? Read the packages to determine what the different kinds of sandpaper are used for.

Project

Make sandpaper and explore its properties.

Directions

1. Spread a mixture of glue and water onto brown wrapping paper.

2. Scatter sand lightly and evenly on the surface of the glue. A coarse strainer works well.

3. Allow the glue to dry and and cut the sandpaper into pieces.

4. Use the sandpaper to smooth surfaces of wood blocks. What happens to wood when it is rubbed with sandpaper? What happens to the sandpaper? Which is harder, the wood or the sandpaper? How can you tell?

Materials

• Brown wrapping paper
• Glue and brush
• Sand
• Coarse sifter

Project

Use sandpaper to create an art project with interesting texture.

Directions

1. Pressing heavily, use crayons to draw a picture on the sandpaper.

2. Heat iron to medium-high. Lay newspaper over picture and heat with the iron. Lift and move the iron; do not slide.

3. Carefully lift the newspaper and allow the picture to cool.

Materials

• Sandpaper squares, approximately 8 x 10 inches (20 x 25 cm)
• Crayons
• Newpaper
• Iron

42

Sand Art

Information

For hundreds of years, people from several different cultures around the world have created sand paintings as part of important ceremonies.

Sometimes sand paintings are made directly on the ground and are not intended to last. When the ceremony is over, the wind blows the art away.

Another well-known form of sand art is building sand castles. Sand, water, molds of different shapes, and creativity come together to build beautiful castles on the beach.

Project

Create a sand-art painting.

Materials

- Sand
- A coarse sifter
- Powdered (or liquid) tempera paints
- Pencils, scissors, soft paint brushes
- White craft glue
- Water and containers
- Cardboard piece, 9 x 12 inches (22.86 x 30.48 cm)
- Measuring tablespoon
- Plastic spoons
- Newspaper

Directions

1. Set up work tables covered with newsprint or cloth for this activity.

2. Sift the sand to get rid of any pebbles and debris.

3. To color sand, mix one tablespoon (15 ml) of powdered tempera paint into one cup of sand. Stir until the sand is evenly colored. (If using liquid tempera, stir the paint and sand until evenly colored. Spread it out in a pie pan or shallow carton to dry completely.) Set out separate containers for each color of sand.

4. Draw a large simple design (rainbow, flower, sunburst, ice cream cone, etc.) onto the piece of cardboard. Plan what colors will be used for each section.

5. Spread glue onto one section for the first color. Spoon the selected color of sand onto the glued area. Cover the area completely with a thick layer of sand.

6. Allow the glue to set awhile. Gently tap the excess sand back into the colored sand container. (Tapping excess sand onto a piece of construction paper and then funneling it into the container is easiest and reduces wasted sand.)

7. Brush any loose sand off the cardboard with a dry brush. Glue the next area and apply the second color of sand. Again allow the glue to set and gently tap off excess sand. Continue until the painting is complete.

9. Allow the painting to dry completely overnight. Brush off any sand from places it shouldn't be.

Rock Collecting

Information

People enjoy collecting all kinds of things. From the traditional collections such as coins and stamps to the more rare like antiques, many people enjoy collecting things—especially things that are old. Rocks are the oldest things you can collect; most of them are millions of years old!

As you begin to search for and collect rocks you will see how many different varieties there are. Igneous, sedimentary, or metamorphic—you will notice differences in size, color, texture, and weight.

Most rocks are ordinary and are easy to find. The different qualities in rocks make collecting them a fun, interesting, and educational hobby.

Project

- Make a decorative box for your rock collection.
- Discuss safety rules related to rock collecting.

Directions

1. Reproduce the safety tips discussion page and distribute.

2. Paint inside and outside of the egg carton.

3. After the paint has dried, personalize your collection box by painting your name on top or adding a decoratively-designed name label.

4. Look for rocks near your home, in your neighborhood, or on family trips. Take along a small notebook to record where and when each rock was located.

5. As rocks are found, place identifying labels in the bottom of each egg compartment. If you cannot identify a rock, make a note of where it was found.

Materials

- Egg carton
- Water-soluble acrylic paints (metallic and pearlescent paints are ideal)
- Paint brushes and containers for water
- Scissors
- Self-adhesive labels
- Pens and markers
- Safety tips discussion page, following

Safety Tips for Rock Collectors

Rock collecting is a great hobby. It's inexpensive, exciting, and you almost always find something new and different. These rules will help your rock collecting adventures be safe ones. Be sure to follow each rule every time you go out collecting.

- Always get permission before going onto anyone's private property. Tell the owner what you would like to do and where you want to go. Be courteous and make sure you leave the property without littering. Remember that going onto private property without permission is unlawful.

- Be especially careful if you plan to collect rocks from a stream or brook—running water can be dangerous.

- Don't drink from a pond, stream, or lake. Bring along your own water—and some food!

- Take along a friend—or an adult! It's safer to have someone else along just in case. It's also more fun!

- Make sure your parents know where you are going and when you plan to return.

- Wear protective clothing. You never know what ground plants you may come by. Wear sturdy clothing that covers your arms and legs, shoes with laces, and bring along a pair of gloves to protect your hands. Don't forget safety goggles to protect your eyes if you're chipping at rock.

- Pack your essential tools in a backpack—a geologist's hammer, a magnifying glass, newspapers or zip-type plastic bags for wrapping your rocks, a small notebook, and a pencil for taking rock-finding notes. It's a good idea to include some bandages too.

- Don't worry if you can't identify your rocks. Even geologists have a hard time identifying some rocks! Record the location where you found the rock and the date you found it. Later on, if you learn what type of rock a sample is, you can add that information.

- Stay away from places that may be dangerous. Use good common sense in making decisions. If you think that something or some place might not be safe, JUST DON'T DO IT! Always trust your first instincts and venture only to places known to be safe.

Rock Art

You've collected a ton (well, almost!) of rocks and now what do you do with them?
Here are some ideas that are fun to make and are great hand-made gift ideas!

Painted Rocks

Materials

- Smooth, flat, medium-sized rocks
- Acrylic paints
- Brushes
- Container for water
- Aluminum pie pan
- Clear varnish

Directions

1. Wash your rocks and make sure they are completely dry.

2. Decide on your design, perhaps a vegetable to identify plants in a garden, a rainbow, or HAPPY BIRTHDAY in pretty colors to give to a friend.

3. Working on an aluminum pie plate to catch drips, paint slowly and carefully.

4. Let the paint dry completely. Add a coat of clear varnish to protect the paint.

Rock Paperweight

Materials

- Glass jar with lid
- Water
- Chlorine bleach (to be used by an adult)
- Rocks

Directions

1. Find a jar with an interesting or unusual shape. Be sure the lid closes tightly. Remove all labels.

2. Select a variety of rocks with different colors, sizes, and textures. Wash them well so all sand and debris is removed.

3. Place the rocks in the jar.

4. Fill the jar about three-quarters full with water. Have an adult add bleach to fill the jar (this will keep algae from growing).

5. Close the lid tightly. Wipe the jar dry.

Game Center

Set aside an area of the classroom for these special games with rocks and minerals!

Rock Recall

Preparation:

- Using a marking pen, divide a large sheet of construction paper into three columns. At the top of each column, write the name of a type of rock: *sedimentary, igneous, metamorphic.*
- Cut six small index cards in half. Number the cards one through 12. On each card, write a characteristic of one of the rock types, preparing four cards for each column.
- Prepare an answer key.

To Play:

- Read the cards, placing each card in the column below the name of the type of rock it describes.
- Use the answer key to check your choices.

Stone Sort

Preparation:

- Collect 12 small stone samples. Use references to correctly identify each sample. Use a permanent marker to number the stones one through 12.
- Write the name of one of the stones in the bottom of each of the sections of an egg carton.
- Prepare an answer key.

To Play:

- Examine each stone and place it in the egg carton section that is marked with its name.
- Use the answer key to check your choices.

In the Bag!

Preparation:

- Prepare a tabletop chart listing the characteristics of the three rock types: *sedimentary, igneous, metamorphic.*
- Collect samples of rocks, being sure to include all three types. Place each sample in a paper lunch bag, folding the top over to close. Number the bags.
- Prepare an answer key that lists the type of rock found in each bag.

To Play:

- Without looking, reach inside each bag and try to identify the rock sample by touch. On a sheet of paper, write your guess for each of the numbered bags.
- Use the answer key to check your choices.

World Wide Web

Look in the world wide web to expand your knowledge of rocks and minerals.
Keep in mind that web pages change constantly. The web pages below were active
at publication date but their continued presence is not guaranteed. Just keep
digging and you will be astonished at just how many "gems" you will find!

Address	Content
mineral.galleries.com/minerals/physical	*The Physical Characteristics of Minerals*—this site will provide in-depth information about minerals.
www.rahul.net/infodyne/rockhounds/rockhounds	*Rockhounds Information Page*—direct links for galleries, collecting sites, images, and clubs, all for the rock collector.
www.metronet.com/~hamstra/honors/nature/rocks	*Honors: Rocks & Minerals*—qualify for an Honors award with your knowledge of rocks and minerals.
cte.jhu.edu/techacademy/fellows/brannon/webquest/kmbindex.html	*Rocks & Minerals Detectives*—here are the tools to help students identify rock and mineral samples.
volcanoes.usgs.gov/Products/Pglossary/pglossary	*Photoglossary of Volcanic Terms*—photos of common volcanic rocks as well as formations.

48

© Edupress EP121